MAGNETIC
HIRING

YOUR COMPANY'S SECRET WEAPON TO
ATTRACTING TOP CYBER SECURITY TALENT

RENEE BROWN SMALL

The Difference Press

McLean, VA, U.S.A.

Copyright © Renee Brown Small, 2017

All rights reserved. No part of this book may be reproduced in any form without permission in writing from the author. Reviewers may quote brief passages in reviews.

Published 2017

ISBN: 978-1-52178-344-3

DISCLAIMER

No part of this publication may be reproduced or transmitted in any form or by any means, mechanical or electronic, including photocopying or recording, or by any information storage and retrieval system, or transmitted by email without permission in writing from the author.

Neither the author nor the publisher assumes any responsibility for errors, omissions, or contrary interpretations of the subject matter herein. Any perceived slight of any individual or organization is purely unintentional.

Brand and product names are trademarks or registered trademarks of their respective owners.

Cover Design: Jennifer Stimson

Editing: Cynthia Kane

Author's photo courtesy of Jenn Reid

*For Jason, Justin, Cameron, and Julia -
my biggest and littlest loves.*

TABLE OF CONTENTS

9
Chapter 01
THE DOWNLOW ON CYBER SECURITY RECRUITING

29
Chapter 02
LISTEN AND LEARN

41
Chapter 03
THE RED TAPE OF UNDERSTANDING SECURITY

53
Chapter 04
BECOME A HIRING MANAGER WHISPERER

65
Chapter 05
UNTAPPED POTENTIALS - EXPLORING INTERNAL AND EXTERNAL RECRUITS

75
Chapter 06
EMPLOYEE VALUE PROPOSITION –
PROPOSING THE PROPOSITION

85
Chapter 07
CREATIVE SOURCING

95
Chapter 08
TRUST THE PROCESS – SEAL THE DEAL

103
Chapter 09
MY WISH FOR YOU

109
Resources

111
Acknowledgements

113
About the Author

115
Thank You

116
About Difference Press

118
Other Books by Difference Press

CHAPTER 01

THE DOWNLOW ON CYBER SECURITY RECRUITING

I wrote this book to help you, fellow recruiters, overcome the challenges of recruiting difficult-to-fill cyber security positions. After struggling as a corporate recruiter myself, and learning through trial and error, I am giving you all the shortcuts that I didn't have when working on these roles.

This first chapter outlines all of the various challenges that you will be up against when trying to recruit for cyber security jobs. You will get a glimpse of the many difficulties dealing with candidates, hiring managers, your own human resources business partners, and compensation team. Throughout the book, I will provide solutions for overcoming these challenges. You will then be able to implement these techniques so you can become the rockstar recruiter who is looked at as a strategic partner.

"Why are you calling me for this, *Again*?" says an irate potential cyber security candidate on the phone. "I spoke to someone named Steve yesterday and explained what I do. I'm a forensics engineer *not* a security compliance analyst. I don't know how many times I have to tell you people. Is anyone listening over there? I get a dozen phone calls and e-mails a day with recruiters asking me if I'm interested in a job. I'm definitely not interested in being a security compliance analyst, whatever the hell that means. I swear I feel like I'm talking to a brick wall. You people are clueless!" CLICK.

"Wow," I say out loud to myself. "Did that really just happen? Did someone straight hang up on me?" My recruiter colleague (and buddy), John, is in the cube next to me and overhears me talking to myself. He pokes his head over the top of the cube and gives me a questioning look, "What happened?"

Is this your life? You, the awesome recruiter that you are - or that you were, before recruiting for the cyber security department at your company. That was me a few years ago. And it baffled me, and made me think I was a fool.

As an IT recruiter in financial services for the past 10 years, I had my share of challenges. There were times that I had difficult-to-fill open positions, hard to please hiring managers, and a tough HR manager. There were times that my former manager rounded up all of the IT recruiters on a conference call and told us that we "didn't know what the f*ck we were doing". There were times that I spent all-nighters getting candidates ready for a project that needed to be staffed in a few days. So I thought I had seen my fair share of challenges in tech recruiting, until I met my match with cyber security.

You probably already have seen all of the statistics out there. According to a recent Forbes.com article, there are over 200,000 current unfilled cyber security roles in the US, and there will be a global shortage of two million cyber security professionals by 2019. You have probably spent an inordinate amount of time sharing this information with hiring managers. They should be well versed on these stats, but if not, walk into your next recruiting meeting armed with this information, so they understand what you (and they) are up against when you start to recruit for them. The very best managers will have a good understanding of how difficult the search will be and will be true partners in helping you search for the talent that they need.

One of my newest clients, a corporate recruiter at a Fortune 100 company, asked me what he could do to find candidates. He wanted to know where he could post positions and where these folks hang out. He wanted to know the secret to finding these people who seem to be completely hidden. He has been working on some cyber security positions for almost a year now with dismal results. None of it is his fault.

You may be feeling the same way – frustrated that you're trying everything that seems to work for every position that you ever worked on, except the cyber security ones.

First, there are not enough talented individuals to go around. There are over 1 million open cyber security positions worldwide, and that is expected to increase substantially. There is 0% unemployment in the security field. Everyone has a job. So, if there isn't enough talent, and the ones with experience are already working, there is your dilemma.

So you, dear recruiter, are posting positions and going to typical tech job sites to get resumes, and you're realizing that it is a total waste of time. Many of them are old resumes and nobody qualified is applying to your positions.

You're trying to convince your hiring managers to give it a little more time and they are equally frustrated. They want to see results. They have been patient over the last few months but they're becoming increasingly frustrated, and I can understand why. Most of them have no idea what it takes to lure someone out of their current role into a new position and company. They absolutely don't know what you're doing on a day-to-day basis to try to find them qualified people. And when you do find someone, they have a "problem" with the person.

Well have no fear, I'm going to teach you how to uncover hidden talent in the security space. I will teach you where to look for talented professionals and how to approach them, so that you end up with a list of talented people who could be a fit for your roles.

You're an awesome recruiter; cyber security is just *really* hard!

You're an awesome recruiter! I know you are because if you weren't looking to figure this out, you wouldn't be reading this book. You are one of those people who loves a challenge. You have an ego - in a good way - and want to outperform the other recruiters in your team. But this is stumping you. These security roles are keeping you up at night. I get it. I was exactly where you are.

As a tech recruiter who was new to the cyber security industry, recruiting these professionals was frustrating to deal with at first. During a typical tech recruitment cycle, I was able to do standard outreach on Stack Overflow or Dice or LinkedIn and get enough interest to be able to present a slate of qualified, interested candidates to a hiring manager. There were definitely instances where I needed to sell the candidate on why they should leave their current employer to come to the employer that I was working for, but in most cases, it was a relatively simple recruitment process.

When I stepped into cyber security, I faced a rude awakening and I know you are facing the same. I was recruiting in the Washington, DC metro area, which is the center of cyber security in the US. There are a few other states and metro areas that are hotbeds for needing talent, as well. Go to **magnetichiring.com** for a list of cities, states, and metro areas with the highest concentration of cyber security jobs. These areas have many more jobs than they have the talent available to support the job openings, so you will have to fight tooth and nail to find someone for a position. If you are recruiting in other towns, there may be more candidates than available positions, but it's still nowhere near an easy search.

You will extend many offers that won't get accepted

You are probably sitting at your desk right now scratching your head at the fact that you "locked up" your candidate, Anthony. You asked all the right questions. You confirmed that he had spoken with his wife about the position. He thought the position would be a great next step in his career. You asked him how the interview went and he thought it was great. He thought the team was a good fit and that the role was perfect for him. You're doing everything on your "Recruiter 101" checklist and all seems to be going well. You ask him what you need to do to make an offer attractive to him so that he will take it. He gives you his requests. He wants to work remotely and wants extra vacation time. He needs to be reimbursed for the training courses that he takes to stay up to date in the security field. Of course, he needs more money, as well.

You take all of his requests and socialize them with the HR business partners and the hiring managers. They typically wouldn't entertain all of these requests, but since this was a difficult-to-fill position that has been open for 4 months, maybe they will. You go to work. You meet with all of the stakeholders and see if you can get them to move forward. After a few days, they all say YES! Victory! You are ready to proceed with the offer to Anthony.

You call Anthony on the phone. You're excited. You can't wait to tell him that all of his requests have been met and ask him for his start date. Anthony doesn't answer, so you leave a voicemail and wait for him to respond. A day goes by and no Anthony. What the what?? You start to get an inkling that something isn't going right. You call again and finally reach him. He apologizes for not returning your call sooner. He was with a client. Ok, you calm down and tell him about the exciting news. You were able to meet all of his requests and you have an offer for him. In your head you say to yourself, "It's an offer he can't refuse."

Anthony graciously acknowledges your offer, but then tells you he needs to compare it to the other offers he's entertaining. He'll get back to you in 3 days. WHAT?

Ultimately, Anthony turns down the offer and you're back to square one.

You are literally shaking your head. Who on God's green earth wouldn't take that offer? You are witnessing the world of the in-demand cyber security professional first hand. Cyber security professionals don't need the offer. They already have 3 or 4 other offers to compare. They are literally the rockstars of the IT industry right now, and they are in a candidate's market. They can make requests that other IT candidates couldn't even think about asking for. And most of the time they get what they're asking for.

I equate them to the house on the market that everyone wants in the middle of a seller's market. What happens? The house gets an offer on it ,and then someone else bids higher and the next person does the same. The next thing you know, a $300K house is now getting offers for $400K. Welcome to cyber security recruiting.

So here's the deal; I will show you how to stack the chips in your favor, so you have a better chance of the candidates accepting your offer. And even if they don't accept, you will have prepped yourself and your hiring manager for that possibility.

Why are there more than 1 million cyber security positions open?

You may be wondering how this even happened. How did we get to a place where there are over 1 million unfilled security positions worldwide? Well, over the past few years there has been an abundance of companies and nation states being hacked. If you live in the US, some of the most recognized security breaches have been with Target, Sony, JP Morgan Chase, LinkedIn, Yahoo, and TJX Companies, parent company of T.J. Maxx, HomeGoods and Marshalls. The Target stores' security breach during Black Friday of 2013 was one of the largest at the time to affect the general consumer, since many had purchased something from a Target store. In this instance, attackers were able to get access to the credit card information in Target's database and proceeded to download all of that credit card data. This meant that everyone who had purchased anything from a Target store during this time using a credit card had essentially had their credit card stolen. Not only did this have an effect on consumer confidence, it also tanked Target's stock. Ouch. Target had to eventually pay out $116 million to settle several lawsuits to banks and consumers over the breach.

Many of us remember the Sony security breach. This happened in 2014 and was unprecedented because it was the first time that a nation state, North Korea, hacked into a US corporation. The Sony employees were shown a screen of skulls and bones when they opened their laptops and turned on their computers. This was the way to show the entire company that they had been hacked. The unreleased movie, Annie, had been stolen and put on the black market before it was fully edited. The rumor was that Sony was planning a movie about the president, and North Korea didn't approve of the way their president was being portrayed so they took down Sony. This showed the level of sophistication that was being used by hackers, and that it was nation states doing this and not just individuals.

JP Morgan Chase had a major security breach in 2014 that exposed over 83 million consumer and small business names, addresses, and emails, making it one of the biggest security breaches in history according to Reuters. JP Morgan Chase is pretty secure, however, they had a third party website that all of their employees used to register for a charitable walkathon. This system was compromised, and hackers were able to gain access to JP Morgan's network.

There are many more examples out there but with these major companies being breached, the general public is now seeing how serious the world of cyber security is. According to cyberscoop.com, the industry is forecasted to grow from $75 billion in 2015 to $170 billion by 2020. With this uptick in growth and major breaches comes an influx of job opportunities in the field.

The candidates hate you and think you suck…maybe they don't hate you but they dislike your recruitment methods

I spend a ridiculous amount of time on LinkedIn. It's my social media of choice since an abundance of my clients and candidates are on there. I recently read a multi-part series of articles titled "How to Hire a Ronin Chang" by a cyber security professional who was writing an open letter to recruiters, because he was annoyed at the amount of requests he receives for roles that don't fit his expertise, as well as the questions recruiters ask him to complete via email or social media that most people would never do (including asking for social security numbers)! He proceeded to vent about the fact that most recruiters don't even view his profile or approach him about jobs that he did years ago that he would never consider doing now. In one of the multi-part articles, he shares that after he wrote his first article, many recruiters reached out to him to understand more and learn about how to recruit a cyber security professional.

This post got multiple likes and comments, mostly from cyber security professionals complementing the article and saying that he was "spot on" in describing their day to day experiences with recruiters. This may be a surprise to you, but I wasn't surprised one bit. As someone who made the transition to cyber security and worked in a Security Operations Center (SOC), I learned firsthand about the "annoying, lazy recruiters" who bombarded my peers every day. I would speak with colleagues, and they would come to me as the "HR person" in the team and ask what was wrong with the people in my profession. Welp. They wanted to understand why we weren't more thorough, and why we would waste time emailing them about positions that didn't match their skills. They wanted to know why we would keep pestering them after they declined or ignored the email or request to connect on LinkedIn. They pretty much thought we were a bunch of idiots! Ouch.

Later in this book, I will teach you how to be the recruiter that the cyber folks seek out when they're ready to make a move. Just like they are your rockstar candidate, you will be their rockstar recruiter and confidante. They will be so appreciative that they found someone who "gets it" that they will come to you for market intel, will ask your opinion when it comes to fair salary ranges, discuss their career challenges, and more. You will become their career coach, and they will LOVE you. When you're looking to fill a position, they will be your go-to person for referrals. You will learn how to make long lasting friendships with cyber security professionals.

I have no idea what these skill sets mean. What's the difference between a security engineer and a SOC analyst anyway?

You are likely trying to understand the full landscape of the cyber security job titles and what they all mean. This can be tricky and frustrating since the same title may mean different things at different companies. The titles are also things you may have never heard of before. I remember saying "incidence response" instead of "incident response" and got many chuckles from managers and candidates.

When you visit magnetichiring.com, I will break down the org charts, titles, and roles and responsibilities into layman's terms so when you're speaking to candidates and managers, you'll be able to understand what it is they're doing on a day to day basis. This will help you quickly separate various security professionals from others. This will also help you when you are submitting candidates to hiring managers. The hiring managers will see that you have a firm grasp of what they do on a daily basis. This will also totally score you points with candidates who will feel like you "get them" when you can translate what they do and speak with them somewhat on their level. All of this will help you get a high level view of a security department and how it works, so you can win points with the hiring managers, candidates, and your HR higher ups.

Best place to work, so what?

Is your company a "Best Place to Work"? If so, great. If not, it doesn't really matter. Have you been on the phone with a candidate touting what a great place to work your company is? You're telling the candidate that you have an awesome gym on premises and an amazing cafeteria. And guess what, the candidate can even work from home a day or two per week. Wow. And you are getting dead silence on the other end of the phone? Or, you're telling a cyber security candidate that your company is a best place to work, and they say "ok, and so…?"

My most difficult recruiting task was at a company that had a bad reputation at the time. Nobody wanted to work there even though they were a "Best Place to Work". What I learned very quickly was enlightening. People definitely cared about the name of the company and some of the perks, but telling someone you have an awesome cafeteria, prior to learning that the candidate is working remotely 100% of the time and has gourmet lunches in the comfort of his own home, makes you look like you're more focused on your company than you are on the candidate. You'll want to learn as much as you can from the candidate prior to sharing the opportunities that you have, so you can determine if any of the positions you have will even be a fit for the person on the other end of the phone or email.

Have you ever had a candidate ask you about the intricacies of the job and you can't give her a true answer because you really don't know them yourself? So you give something vague, and the person gets disinterested.

We will go through this very important step of learning about the candidates' wants and selling in the parts of the job that will be most important to them.

My company is like a D-list celebrity. Nobody wants to work here

It's easy to recruit talent to work for Apple, Google, Uber, and Amazon. All types of technology professionals are clamoring to get inside these companies. They want to work in a fast-paced environment at a company with a start-up feel. If you're a recruiter in an environment like this, I would imagine that you're able to get a good response rate from the individuals that you reach out to.

Now what if you work at a D-list company with no brand? This is where the real fun begins. If you are working for a company that no one has ever heard of, or a company that has a bad reputation, you're in for a treat. It will be much harder to convince someone to leave their Fortune 500 company's information security job to come and work for your D-list company, but it IS possible.

Even worse is if you have a hiring manager that wants a candidate from a grade A company. You will have to bring this manager from outer space and back to earth, and then explain why that will likely not happen. You will be setting the manager's expectations by asking a variety of questions, so the manager will convince themself that it's more realistic not to go after the cream of the crop candidates.

Your hiring managers will sing your praises to your HR manager. You will learn how to become a trusted advisor and coach to your hiring managers. They will defer to you because you will be able to share market data, as well as real time information on what's happening in the market with companies and candidates. You will be able to coach them with interviewing and how to sell the company and role. You will be a confidante and trusted colleague, and not an "order taker" as many of them say about HR recruiters and HR business partners.

Are you disappointed in yourself?

What keeps you up at night? Do you envision a hiring manager telling your boss that you are not meeting their expectations? Are they riding you day and night to fill their positions and looking exasperated when you bring them candidates that you think could be a fit, but they completely shut down?

If this sounds like your situation, you are not alone. I was exactly in your shoes. I was staying up at night, thinking and working, to get candidates for the managers. My reputation was on the line, and I didn't want the hiring managers telling my HR manager how I couldn't cut the mustard. Another lady in my department had gotten negative feedback from a director in the company, and although she wasn't at fault, it ultimately led to her demise. A few other recruiters had lost their jobs for similar internal client complaints. I couldn't afford to be in that situation. I was sinking, and I was desperately trying to get myself above water.

I was disappointed that I had gotten to this point. I couldn't believe that I was dealing with this at this point in my life and career. I was above this... well that's what I told myself. If you are feeling this way, you are not alone. This industry and this group of professionals is an interesting bunch. You will adapt to what makes them tick and come out of this situation, a star! You will be rewarded by hiring managers and executives for solving their biggest problems. You will be able to get a promotion. I was able to move into a bigger role within the cyber security department after my success. You will be able to do similar if that is what you choose to do. If you follow the simple steps in this book, you will kick ass, get that promotion, and move out of the grind that you're in! I believe in you!

KEY TAKEAWAYS

This chapter outlined the various reasons cyber security positions are so difficult to fill. It also described the challenges that you will face while recruiting for these positions.

CHAPTER 02

LISTEN AND LEARN

"Life's biggest rewards come from the biggest challenges."

– GREG BEHRENDT

In this chapter, I will share my career experiences in human resources, technology recruiting, and as a cyber security program manager and security operations center analyst. This combination of experiences makes me equipped to give advice on this topic from both a recruiter's perspective, as well as the security professional's view.

You are probably asking yourself the following questions. Who are you to give me this advice? What qualifications and experience do you have? And ultimately, why should I listen to you? These are all questions you should be asking, and I would be asking the same if I were in your shoes right now.

My background is unique, and I have multiple types of experiences that make me the person you absolutely want to listen to when it comes to this subject.

I was in your exact shoes six years ago. I had been hired as a corporate recruiter at a Fortune 50 financial services company to focus mostly on technical recruiting. A few months into my role, I was given the information security department as an area I was going to support. At the time, I had no idea what information security was or what the department did. I was also put on the executive recruiting team to work on some executive positions that were Vice President level and above. I know in some financial institutions, VPs can have only a few years of experience. This wasn't the case at this company. The VPs were officers of the company, usually with a minimum of 10 years experience leading a department of about 100 people.

Prior to working as a corporate recruiter at this organization, I had an additional 10 years of corporate and agency recruiting experience. Most of it was doing technical recruiting for financial services companies. In addition, I did recruiting in the education sector, as well as recruiting outside of technology to include finance, audit, actuarial, HR and more. To summarize, I had filled hundreds of positions in many environments over the years in the tech recruiting space. I have seen almost everything there is to see when it comes to recruiting. So I was baffled when the cyber security recruiting project stumped me.

I've never been one to shy away from a challenge. Like you, I was an awesome recruiter. I had hiring managers and candidates of all levels singing my praises. I had an SVP write a note to my boss praising me for filling a difficult-to-fill role for a scientist in a few months that had been open for over a year with no results.

I was on track to having a stellar year with solid metrics and performance ratings. And then I was handed the information security department that was in shambles. This challenging situation was going to upend my performance, and at the time I had mixed emotions. I was annoyed that I was given this nightmare of a group while my peers were working on the simple open positions. I was embarrassed that with all my prior experience, I couldn't crack this nut. I was tired from staying up all night when my first baby wasn't yet one year old with a husband who traveled and worked long hours when he wasn't traveling. I was a wreck!

I remember being yelled at (over e-mail) by a director in the information security department. He was upset that I didn't give him a report before the deadline and sent the information up to his boss, the VP of the group. I was so nervous and embarrassed when that happened. I pulled an all-nighter to get them the information, and I didn't even get a "thank you". Thinking about this even now, years later, still gives me the chills.

I was eventually able to crack the code for recruiting these difficult cyber security professionals, and it was all sunshine and rainbows from there. I won many company awards; one was a large monetary award that is typically only for information technology professionals, and the IT leadership team made the decision to give it to me. I was praised constantly for going above and beyond in such a challenging environment.

The Chief Information Security Officer (CISO) and two of his directors with the most open positions included me in their strategy sessions. They got me awards and they continued to share the positive impact that I made on the team.

The Chief Technology Officer (CTO) of the company offered me a position in his department to focus on staff planning for the entire IT department, which was a huge jump from being a recruiter and just focusing on recruiting activities.

A year later, I was offered a position as a program manager in the information security department working directly with most of the people I recruited! The trajectory had been amazing. I never thought that I would end up in the group that I struggled to find talent for. I was working for my favorite hiring managers. I was on cloud nine!

Read on, and you will learn how to position yourself to stand out from the crowd. You will learn how to stand out as the alpha recruiter who your HR manager and the hiring managers will want to quickly move up the ladder. You will soon step into your new promotion and be rewarded for the rockstar that you are.

My life as a cyber security professional

How do you make the jump from cyber security recruiter to cyber security professional? It's actually not as difficult as you may think. I believe that there is a huge advantage for HR professionals in cyber security. According to workforce.com, in cyber security, sometimes the focus is too heavy on the technology and not enough on the human factors. Because HR professionals are so focused on the human and their behaviors, we become an asset to the cyber security team.

Even if you have no interest in becoming a security professional long term, it's always good to get out of your comfort zone and do a rotation in an information security department if possible. It makes you a more valuable employee when you can bring experiences that your peers don't have.

After working on filling the information security positions in that company, many in the information security leadership team viewed the creative way I solved those problems as an asset. I continuously researched what other companies were doing and by bringing those ideas to the table, no stone was unturned. Some of the ideas seemed pretty outrageous, however, some landed and worked out well. This showed leadership that I was a risk taker and did what I needed to do to get the job done.

When I got to the security department, it was eye opening. I was a complete fish out of water initially.

I had no idea what I was doing! It took me a while to get acclimated to the way things were being done, what everyone was doing, and why they were doing those things. It was a struggle. I was about to have my second baby and I was ready to pop. I was learning a new role and was actually in awe of the opportunity that I was being given. I didn't want to mess up, but secretly, in my head, I was a disaster.

As I got more comfortable with the team, I started to learn what made them tick. This was the most interesting aspect for me since I had seen so much turnover in the different groups over the past few years. I learned about what was exciting to them and what made them dread their work. I saw what made them frustrated and how a new person who joined the team could have such an effect on team morale - either positive or negative. I saw who the team members respected as their peers and why they respected those colleagues. I also heard them make comments about senior management and how far removed management was from what was their reality.

I picked up ques daily about them and this was fascinating for me. I don't know what was more interesting, the actual information security work or observing the interactions of the team members. At the time, I wished every recruiter and HR person who had a security group could see this. It was amazing to watch.

I will give you the Cliff Notes version of what I learned. I will be walking you through what I saw as a security professional, sitting next to these folks, and learning what made them happy one day and ready to quit the next.

What I learned in each role. Blending the two roles.

The fun part about being an HR professional in information security is that team members come up with hypothetical questions that you know aren't hypothetical at all. I got all kinds of requests from them on how things worked in HR. They wanted the inside scoop and I happily shared the information I had. They wanted to understand promotions, salary structures, benefits, and more. Then when they were thinking about leaving (they obviously wouldn't tell me this outright but I could tell by the types of questions they asked), they would question the duration of benefits and eligibility for rehire should they leave the company.

The most significant takeaway for me was understanding the psyche of a security professional. Especially the millennial ones. It was fascinating to see how quickly they made decisions and why they made the decisions that they did. To see someone perfectly happy in their role do a 180 and suddenly resign was so interesting to watch. This experience has helped me when coaching my clients on how to not only recruit security professionals but also how to retain them - the much bigger issue.

My story as an executive search and HR consultancy CEO

As the CEO of a cyber security HR company, I consult recruiters in the field, my former self, every day. Sometimes it's like deja vu when I speak with you all, because I truly feel like I'm talking to myself six years ago. I feel your anxiety when discussing candidates. I feel your hurt when you think you have someone for a job and they decline. I can hear the confusion in your voice sometimes when you're trying to describe what the hiring manager is seeking in candidates.

As I coach clients, I share the pitfalls of trying to recruit cyber security professionals the way you would DBAs, project managers, or some other IT folks. My clients gain more confidence knowing that many of the offers that they extend won't be accepted – and that is ok. They can now coach hiring managers on what's realistic in the marketplace and what skill sets will come at what price points. They even can recommend alternatives to trying to hire full-time employees for certain roles.

I wrote this book to help you gain the knowledge that you need so you can confidently meet with your hiring managers, HR managers, and candidates. You will be able to understand each one's perspective, and share with them what role they each will need to play for successful recruitment efforts.

At the end of the book, you will be able to see what is important to each constituent and what you need to do to help them achieve their goal. Each person wants to be successful, and it's your role to make that happen for all of them. You will be able to conduct what's now a cacophony into a beautiful orchestra.

KEY TAKEAWAYS

1. Listen to a recruiter who has had experience in cyber security - a tech recruiter who doesn't work on cyber security roles won't have the same insight. You'll also want to listen to reputable headhunters who are speaking to managers and candidates on a daily basis.

2. Try to do a rotation in a cyber security department if possible. You will gain enormous insight even sitting in the same room as some of the cyber security team members one day per week.

CHAPTER 03

THE RED TAPE OF UNDERSTANDING SECURITY

Julia had scheduled a strategy meeting with a hiring manager, Lawrence, for a security engineering role. She reviewed the job description, did some Google searches on terms she didn't know, and wrote some questions down that she was going to ask him. Her list looked something like this:

1. How many years of experience should the person have in these listed skills?

2. Are these certifications listed a "must have"?

3. Is there flexibility in the work schedule?

4. Is this a nationwide search or do the candidates need to be local?

As soon as the conference call started, the manager, Lawrence, jumped in with his requirements and didn't let her get a word in edgewise. He wanted 5 years experience in Linux as an expert and 2 years experience in AWS. The person needs to have a CISSP certification and that was non-negotiable. He would prefer that the person had a cloud certification as well. The person had to come into the office everyday. There is no remote work arrangement in this role. Oh, and their group was "very picky" on the personality types of candidates they were seeking.

Julia's head was spinning. She thought to herself, "This is nuts. I don't understand half of these technologies or what they mean or even if this kind of skill set is out there in the marketplace."

If you're like Julia, you're not alone. The information security field is fast growing and ever-changing. A technology or tool that was in use a year ago may be obsolete today. A company will continue to re-organize their departments to align with what is best for the business. For example, there has been a recent push for portions of information security to be put under the risk management divisions in large companies so that information security risk can be looked at with all different types of business risk.

At **magnetichiring.com,** there are sample org charts of different information security departments.

Know your company

Lawrence, the hiring manager that Julia was speaking with, was completely out of touch with the reality of getting talent with this type of skill set. For most security roles, it is a candidate's market. The candidate is getting dozens of phone calls and e-mails daily from recruiters, and this is not an exaggeration. To ask for someone with this skill set, education, and experience to come into your office every day, without an option for some remote work flexibility, is virtually impossible.

Quite often managers are not aware of what is happening in the marketplace when they request various skill sets. They may be getting a directive from their higher up, who could be even more clueless about how many people out there even have these skills. Or that a person with one set of skills likely won't have another, and they are really asking for two different types of people. Of course you probably wouldn't know this either. Even as someone who is immersed in this field, I'm learning something new daily, and I ask managers and candidates all the time to explain certain skill sets to me so I can understand what's going on in the market. It's like if a manager wanted to hire a recruiter with extensive technical recruiting experience but the technical recruiter must also have a JD because they need an attorney on the team. Are there people out there with that experience? Maybe a few. Is it realistic to ask for this skill set? Nope. It's probably faster and cheaper to hire a tech recruiter and an HR attorney. Unbeknownst to you, this is sometimes what you're up against when trying to hire a combination of skill sets that don't typically mix.

A few things went awry with how this conversation with Lawrence started off. Julia was unable to provide a trusted advisor approach and ended up like an "order taker", because Lawrence just showed up with a laundry list of requirements and requests. Julia needs to rehearse her intake form and script so as not to fall prey to being an order taker. She may not have known that the skill sets don't align and that's ok, it will come in time, but she should know the basics. There are major challenges recruiting in this space, and that regardless of what a manager is seeking, the certification requirements and the inflexible work arrangement will make it even more difficult to attract candidates.

How important is security to your org?

If you are a new recruiter in the security space, there are certain things that you'll need to learn about your company up front. Some of this will be obvious and some will take some deeper digging to determine how best to approach the candidates you're seeking. Every company will say that security is their top priority, although that isn't always the case. Some industries and companies are more conscientious than others when it comes to cyber security.

Let's take the financial services industry as an example. They have been at the forefront of cyber security for obvious reasons. Banks don't want to be breached and have customers doubt their ability to keep their financial assets safe. They need to continue to stay ahead of the trends, or at a minimum keep up, when it comes to cyber security. They are also regulated by the federal government and are mandated to have certain criteria in place to stay compliant. So, it is extremely important for them to have top cyber security talent. This is also true for the retail, energy, medical, technology industries, and any organization with a lot of intellectual property.

There are other organizations that have an information security department because it may be mandated or it's a nice to have, but the risk of not having one is not that big of a deal.

You're probably wondering, "So what?" The reason why this is important is because of the talent. The best and brightest talent wants to work for companies on the cutting edge of security. They want to keep and grow their skills on the latest technologies and keep up with the latest trends. This is going to happen at those forward-thinking companies. The first questions potential candidates will ask are about the company culture and the latest projects that the company is working on. They will also go on sites like Glassdoor to see what is being said about the company. You will need to be able to explain, at a high level, why they should consider leaving their current job and moving to whatever job opening you are recruiting on. There must be some intrigue or else they will not be interested.

I recently had a conversation with 2 prospective candidates about a Fortune 100 company I'm recruiting for right now. One prospect told me that he has heard a lot of negative things about the company and their reputation is shot. He said he was going to look on Glassdoor to see if there was anything new. I had to agree with him that some pockets of the company had bad reputations, but this particular group that I was working with didn't operate like the rest of the company – that they had new leadership. Another prospect, who is currently in one of the hottest companies in his field, told me that this project and company I was recruiting for didn't sound intriguing and wasn't something he wanted to work on for the next year. Ouch. This is a reality and I make sure that I take information like this back to the hiring managers - especially when they think that their project or role is so fascinating and wonder why they can't get talent from top companies that have the talent they are seeking. When I shared this information with the hiring manager, he sounded so surprised that candidates were saying this. It was even eye opening to him, and he was very attuned to the market and the fact that the candidates had their pick of the litter.

This leads into discussing the types of candidates a manager is seeking. As shared, some companies are at the forefront of cyber security and some are lagging behind. If there is misalignment with the type of candidate pool that the manager wants, you will struggle to find anyone who will be interested in the job. We will discuss this more in depth in a later chapter, and I will share how to have your managers assess why they think they need "rockstars" from specific industries or companies, especially when they have neither the compensation nor exciting projects to attract or retain this type of person.

This will sound pretty basic, but you'll need to Google your company or set a Google alert everyday and see what news is being published. Frequently review sites like Glassdoor to see what current and former employees are saying about the company. Trust that the candidates will do the same. As soon as you share the company that you're working with, they will quickly try to find information.

The first step in being able to pitch an opportunity is knowing your company. Is it a huge company that everyone knows with a great reputation? Or maybe a huge company with not the best reputation? Is it a startup with no brand recognition but doing phenomenal work in a niche? Is it a large company that purchased a smaller company so the person gets the combination of a startup feel with big company funding?

The answers to these kinds of questions will help you frame your initial conversation with the candidates. The candidates will also want to know more about the management team, the actual work, and their specific environment. This is called the Employee Value Proposition (EVP). We will review this in detail in a later chapter, and I will show you how to write an amazing EVP that will get candidates excited about the opportunities you have to offer.

Cyber Security 101 (Cyber security for dummies and more)

Let's face it. This world of information security is confusing. And most of us aren't technical. We are recruiters. So, unless you worked in an area of information security prior to recruiting this group of talent, it's hard to understand what these folks do on a daily basis. This is why I recommend you get a baseline understanding of what cyber security is, how it started, and how it's become one of that fastest growing industries in the world. By understanding this at a high level, you'll be able to have an intelligent conversation with both hiring managers and prospective candidates. You will also start to understand how some of the different roles fit together and what's most important in your organization.

There are a number of Cyber Security for Dummies books that are free on Amazon and provide an intro to cyber security. A quick Google search and Youtube search will provide a plethora of Security 101 books, articles, and videos that give an overview of what security is and why it's important. Be prepared going into meetings with managers and candidates by getting as up to date as possible with what's going on in the world of information security. At **magnetichiring.com,** I share a list of the websites that security professionals frequent to get their news and information. This research and knowledge will give you a leg up against other recruiters in your company, as well as other companies who have no clue about the information security space.

If you are in a company that offers tuition reimbursement or professional development training, take advantage of that. It will benefit you greatly to take an intro course to cyber security. Again, having access to a trainer or professor in the field who can answer questions and give clarity to an area that can be confusing is invaluable. In a training course, you will be able to get a good overview of the latest happenings in security. You will also be able to network with all of the folks in the class as most of them are soon-to-be cyber security professionals, and they will be happy to network with a recruiter with whom they can ask questions.

KEY TAKEAWAYS

In this chapter, you learned about knowing your organization in order to be able to recruit talent more seamlessly:

1. Determine how important security is to your organization.

2. Do due diligence on the perception your company has in the eyes of candidates.

3. Get a basic understanding of security.

CHAPTER 04

BECOME A HIRING MANAGER WHISPERER

In this chapter, I will show you how to understand what's happening in your hiring manager's head when they have a position to fill. I will give you steps to earn their trust as an advisor and tips for effective expectation setting.

James schedules a 15-minute meeting with his manager, Maryanne, on Monday morning. Mondays are typically a rough day for the team. Along with the standard day's work and all of the incidents that need to be cleaned up from the weekend, there are reports due that must be completed before the end of the day. Maryanne wonders what could be on James' mind since this is a day that he knows she is slammed. If it were anyone else, she would try to reschedule until tomorrow but James is one of

Maryanne's top performers, so she definitely wants to hear what he has to say.

When the meeting time comes, James looks a little bit nervous and so Maryanne starts to get nervous. She starts by telling him to have a seat and says she's curious to hear what he wants to discuss. James begins by saying, "I want to thank you for the opportunity; however, I'm taking a role at a new company and will be handing in my resignation. I'm sad to go but this is a very exciting opportunity for me to grow my skill set and leadership capabilities."

Maryanne musters up a plastic smile and congratulates him – even though deep down she is pissed! She tells him it seems sudden and asks if there is anything that could be done to keep him. He tells her there is nothing that can keep him, his decision is made up and he will be leaving. So she tells him to e-mail a resignation letter that she can send to HR, and she will get back to him to discuss a transition plan.

When James leaves Maryanne's office, she puts her head in her hands. This is totally not what she needs at this critical time. She is already down 2 staff members who transferred to different departments within the past 60 days and can't seem to keep up with the projects that she has on her plate. James is one of her top performers. He's the type of person who doesn't need any guidance or direction. She can't believe that she's about to lose him.

Maryanne puts in a call to her HR business partner, Amy, to let Amy know that she is going to be down another person. Amy sympathizes with her and asks her what she can do to help. Maryanne says what HR could do is put a priority on hiring the people that she has lost. She's swamped, and it seems as though HR can't get it right when it comes to sending her candidates that are a fit for her positions. They are making more work for her than anything else by having her screen through resumes of people who have absolutely no skills that matched any of her backfills.

Amy calls Fred to her office. Fred is the recruiter working on Maryanne's positions. Amy asks Fred how it's been going working with Maryanne. Fred says he's frustrated. He's sent Maryanne candidates but she's swamped, and she doesn't get back to him with feedback so he doesn't know if he's hitting the mark when it comes to the people he's sending her. It also seems to be a very difficult skill set. He's posted the position in the usual places to get tech talent and he's not getting many bites.

Amy realizes that she needs to get Fred and Maryanne in a meeting as soon as possible. Maryanne is swamped, likely doing the jobs of herself and her staff members who are now gone. She is going to be under much more pressure since she is now going to be down a third person. She believes that HR has no idea what types of people she's looking for. Fred has been doing his job and sending her people but he hasn't gotten any feedback, so he has no idea if any of those people could be a fit. Both are frustrated and this miscommunication isn't productive for any of the parties involved.

The hiring manager

As recruiters, we tend to wonder what the problem is with hiring managers. More often than not, we get frustrated with their crazy requests, their lack of responsiveness, and how they act like we can manufacture candidates with all of their wild skill set requests. We feel like they don't treat us as trusted advisors or business partners, the way they treat their accounting and finance partners or their attorneys. It can feel like we are just a bunch of order takers.

It's true. Some of the hiring managers that I've come across have been nightmares. They will act like recruiters are the worst people they have ever interacted with. They make it seem like we are bothering them by trying to help them fill their positions, and they find fault with everything we do.

We also know they aren't all like that and some managers are complete pleasures to work with and partner with. They are partners and understand the level of effort that goes into getting them the right talent at the right time. They respect our opinions and view us as trusted business partners who understand what's going on in the job market and what needs to be done to bring top talent to the table.

If you've never had to hire a person before, it's hard to understand what a hiring manager is going through when they have to backfill a position. Not only are they doing their own job, they, (along with their team members) are likely overworked as they pick up the slack for those no longer with the group. On top of doing their day job and more, they have to dedicate time to looking for a replacement who will fit in with the team, who has the appropriate skills, and the right personality. This is a stressful and difficult time for everyone involved.

Get the hiring manager on your side

One of the easiest and fastest ways to get the hiring manager on your side is to empathize with them. Let them know that you understand how stressful this process can be. Acknowledge that they are under the gun to get someone in the spot quickly and you are going to do what you need to do to make that happen. Also, provide them some information about what's going on in the marketplace for the types of roles they're hiring for. This information could include articles on hiring in your area or information on how many people in the market have a certain skill set and certification. By approaching a hiring manager in this way, you are automatically setting yourself apart from the other recruiters who have interacted with them. They are already viewing you as someone who is in partnership with them to alleviate their stressful situation.

Then you want to ask questions about the role that show you're looking for a long-term fit for their group. Ask questions like: What are the success factors for someone in the role? How can this person earn you a high performance review at the end of the year? What were the strengths and weaknesses of the people you're trying to backfill? If you could wave a magic wand, what type of person would be sitting in that seat tomorrow?

When you ask questions like these, they realize that you are trying to get them someone that will make them shine. Someone who lifts some of the pressure they have. They will look to you as a source of support and value your opinion.

Next, you want to explain what you know about the current job market for the type of role they're looking to fill. A quick Google search will give you a bit of insight as to what's happening if you don't already know.

For example, I recently received a group of cloud security positions where the manager wanted people to have experience in Splunk and experience in Amazon Web Services (AWS). I had already had experience recruiting people with Splunk experience and it was extremely difficult. I could share with the hiring manager how difficult it was going to be, since I had just done a similar search. In regards to the AWS role, I had not recruited on a role like that before, so I did some research to determine a rough estimate of how many people nationwide had those skills. I also looked at how many job openings requested those skills. I was able to come to the meeting with some metrics, so when I told the manager that it was going to be a really tough search, I could give him reasons why (that there were only X people in the market with this skill and there are Y job openings requesting it). When you can share facts with the manager, they see you as a value and not someone who is trying to put up barriers as to why they can't get what they want.

How do you recruit a real "rock star" or "pop star"

I don't know what it's like to be a talent agent in the sports & entertainment world, but after watching Jerry Maguire or a few episodes of Entourage, I can imagine how crazy it can get. What's it like when you try to recruit the hottest talent in town to be a part of your project? As I'm writing this book, the hottest artists on the Billboard 100 are Future, Bruno Mars, The Weeknd, Chainsmokers, Rihanna, Drake and Adele. Think about what you would need to do to get an artist like one of these to be a part of your project. How many times do you have to call Drake's manager? How do you even get his manager's phone number? How much money do you have to offer him? Of all the projects that he's being bombarded with, what would make yours stand out? Ultimately, why would Drake want to work with you?

Now, these stars are in the top 10 on the billboard charts this week, so yes, they are probably out of reach for most projects but what about the next level or two down? Do you think they are also getting bombarded with projects? They may get even more requests, because people may think it's more attainable and economical to try to get someone who hasn't been a Super Bowl half-time act!

This is a microcosm of the cyber security talent pool. As previously noted, there are over 1 million positions open worldwide without enough professionals to fill them. There is 0% unemployment and a lot of cyber security folks can double up and work a full-time gig plus multiple side projects.

With all of this said, they are truly the pop stars of IT. It's a candidate's market, and they can pick and choose who to even respond to if they decide to respond to anyone at all. So imagine being Adele and getting a phone call from someone who knows you're a singer but has no idea what types of songs are your forte and has never listened to your music. Huh? What?

Understand the landscape

Since I have straddled both the HR and cyber security sides, I've always heard from some irritated cyber professionals who get "annoying" calls from recruiters. Recently, I've seen a number of articles on LinkedIn with cyber security folks complaining about being bombarded with recruiters, some corporate and some agency, who have no idea how to interact with them.

As shared in a previous chapter, one particular guy, Ronin Chang, wrote a 4-part series of articles giving examples of how bad it is for him being bombarded by recruiters. He said that he was so fed up and had so many stories to tell that one article was not enough.

Another article was forwarded to me by my former cyber security director. This was also an article on LinkedIn where an executive level candidate spoke negatively about his agency recruiter and how he should have seen the signs to not work with him or interview for the job that he presented. He also praised a different recruiter who had a specialty in the marketplace and understood what he was seeking.

I provide all of these examples not only for you to understand what you're up against and what a cyber security professional is dealing with from recruiters, but to also keep this information in the forefront of your mind to share with your hiring managers. Everyone on the recruitment team (recruiter, hiring manager, compensation team, HR business partner) should be well versed in the security job market and landscape, so you all know what to expect.

Your hiring manager is a rock star to someone, too

Make your hiring manager one of the pop stars. Tell them that you know they must be bombarded with requests due to their specialty and expertise, and ask them to think about what it takes to get them to respond. What kind of message has to be relayed for them to send an email back to a recruiter or take a phone call with a recruiter? Tell them to remember that is what you're dealing with as you try to recruit people for their role.

You want the manager to see all sides. You want them to understand the battle that you're fighting as you chase down this 0% unemployment, mostly passive talent pool. You also want them to remember what it's like to be in the candidate's position.

KEY TAKEAWAYS

Backfilling a role is stressful for everyone involved - the hiring manager, her team, and the recruitment team.

1. Empathize with the manager.

2. Educate the manager by sharing your expertise about the job market.

3. Approach cyber security professionals like how you would recruit a real pop star.

4. Make your hiring manager a pop star.

CHAPTER 05

UNTAPPED POTENTIALS - EXPLORING INTERNAL AND EXTERNAL RECRUITS

In this chapter, I will outline the various recruitment options for hiring cyber security talent. Some options may include growing talent from within.

Mike is an information security director at a Fortune 500 corporation. He was given multiple audit findings from his internal audit team for not having enough cyber security staff in his department. It was posing a risk to the company to be down so many people in that team. He has reviewed over 80 resumes and has had a number of interviews for his various roles and extended a few offers but nobody has accepted. The other people who interviewed haven't hit the mark in terms of the skill sets that he needs for the team. At this point, he's not being picky, he has a certain criteria that he has to meet and he's at his wits end.

Mike has nothing but praise for Amy, his recruiter. Amy has been a partner in this effort working diligently to find candidates that meet his criteria. She's reached out to over 300 candidates to get to the slate of candidates he has now. She has provided a list of all of the candidates reviewed and screened and how many are just not interested in a new career opportunity. She has been an open book and has shown Mike her notes so he understands exactly what's happening during the recruitment cycle.

Amy agrees that Mike has been a joy to work with but has been dealt a rough hand. Most of his team turned over all at once. Then the audit finding came down and he has been scrambling to keep his head above water. He's made a number of offers that have been turned down. His company went through a scandal a few years ago and their reputation is still pretty bad. Not many people are lining up to work at the organization, especially since most are gainfully employed. Amy has to come up with some creative ways to bring in people to this group.

Both Amy and Mike understand the talent gap in cyber security all too well. Amy does some research and sees that a few employers are having successes by going after people that may not have the exact cyber security technical skills they are seeking but have the soft skills that, as they say, "can't be taught". These companies have looked at people with a "security mindset" and trained them in the technical skills and these recruits have turned out to be fantastic.

Amy takes this research to Mike and presents the case to look for some skills that should be easier to find and easier to recruit. Mike has nothing to lose at this point since nothing else is working. Amy gets approval from her manager to do a pilot recruitment program, but she doesn't go externally. She sets up a program to recruit from within.

The history of security: Recruit From Within.

One of the most enlightening observations when I moved from HR into a security department at a Fortune 100 company was understanding the culture and learning how people got there. I remember having a conversation with one of my colleagues, and he had shared that he started in what would eventually be called the Information Security department over 15 years ago. This was before it was called information security. He told me there were four guys that got pulled from their former jobs to join the new information security group. As I met with more team members, I learned that many had come from backgrounds other than security. Most had been in technology prior to their jobs in information security but some had no IT experience at all. One person had worked on the help desk for a few years before transitioning over to a security operations center (SOC) analyst. Another had been an internal auditor prior to moving into information security. One lady had started her career as a secretary. The department head started his career as a network engineer. And I had my background in HR. More often than not, the folks in this group had skills from other areas before moving into security. Only the more recent college grads and early career hires had started their careers in security.

This nugget of information made me start to research other companies and learn what they were doing with their security departments. Were other companies hiring non-cyber security people and training them in the technical skills needed? How were other companies staffing their security teams? Did they have some magic wand that they were waving, or were they just bringing in staff and training them with the skills necessary? This was intriguing.

Case Studies

One of the hardest skill sets to find right now is in a tool called Splunk. This technology is used to search, monitor, and analyze machine-generated big data. The technology has only been around for 10 years, and the company has exploded in the past few years. As I was learning to use Splunk in my role as a SOC analyst, I worked alongside a guy who worked directly for Splunk. I asked him what skills they look for when they are looking for talent since it's a relatively new technology. He shared that a good Linux admin would make a good Splunk admin because Splunk is built on a Linux platform. A good C++ or Python developer makes a good Splunk developer because it was mostly developed in C++ and Python. So, there you have it. They aren't looking for the exact skill set in the marketplace. It's easier to find a Linux admin or a Python developer than it is to find someone already well versed in Splunk. They are looking for people who have a broader, underlying skill set that can be easily transferred over to their technology.

Northrop Grumman is a leading global security company that started a Cyber Academy in 2011. As detailed on their website, it provides training courses, learning opportunities and career certification pathways for employees and customers to increase their knowledge of cyber security and cyber warfare. The Cyber Academy helps ensure Northrop Grumman has the most knowledgeable, qualified talent available to take on the full spectrum of cyber challenges for its customers.

The way Northrop Grumman stays ahead of the curve with cyber security staff is by training their own, from non-technical courses for novices that are a few hours long to multi-day technical courses for those who are already security experts in their field.

Northrup Grumman also sponsors the Cyber Patriot competition that puts HS and middle school students in a competition so they can play the part of a manager in the middle of a cyber attack.

Sponsoring these types of events helps Northrup start developing talent at a younger age and gets them brand recognition with the students.

If your company is thinking long term, you all can sponsor a competition like this or even sponsor a middle school or high school in your area so that you can start to build a pipeline of talent in the middle school and high school years.

Any company can do this on a smaller scale. Your company doesn't need to have the muscle of a billion dollar corporation to start up a cyber academy or something similar. It can be as simple as identifying internal talent that has baseline skills and then sending them to free training courses. The other option is to provide paid training courses through a host of different training providers that are focused in training people in cyber security. There are a list of free and paid training on magnetichiring.com. Statistics have shown that people who are given the opportunity to continue to learn and grow in their careers are more likely to be retained by the organizations that give them those opportunities. This approach will help your leaders retain staff, which is the other half of the cyber talent challenge.

Grow your own security talent: External hires

Another way to ensure that your company gets the talent that they need is to grow them yourselves. I have seen this done with a number of hard to fill skill sets over the years, in the technology field and in other fields. One company that has had successes with the model on a large scale is PwC. Rather than continuously fight the talent war with trying to attract the same talent, they have gone after veterans and college grads that don't necessarily have STEM (science, technology, engineering, and math) degrees. They provide boot camps to bring these folks in and get them trained in a number of certifications. This has proven to be a major success for them as they attempt to hire 1000 candidates this way.

Symantec has also had success stories bringing in early career talent from a number of organizations. The one I'm most familiar with is Year Up. Year Up's mission is to close the opportunity divide by providing urban young adults with the skills, experience, and support that will empower them to reach their potential through professional careers and higher education. The nonprofit provides a pipeline of young talent for partner companies while delivering a market-driven training program that helps low-income adults launch a professional career.

Year Up finds low-income young adults and trains them for one year. Six months of the training is in the Year Up facilities being trained in a classroom setting in a technical skill and in how to work in a corporation. The other six months is an internship at a company where the interns can utilize the skills that they've recently acquired. Year Up has recently started a cyber security training program where they train young adults who have a high school diploma and may have college credits. Symantec is one of the oldest leaders in the cyber security space. Many of you may know of them from the Norton Antivirus software and check mark that is seen on websites worldwide. The partnership that these two companies have has also proven successful with bringing in untapped talent into corporate environments through internships. This group of young people tends to be extremely motivated and the retention rate is high since this is usually their first opportunity to work in a corporate environment and earn a high paying income.

All of these are ways to think outside of the usual parameters of poaching the same talent over and over again from your competitors. With programs like these in place, your company will be well on its way to closing the security gap in your organization.

KEY TAKEAWAYS

1. A recruiting strategy should include evaluating internal talent that can be trained.

2. Top companies are creating cyber academies or sending current employees to cyber boot camps and other training courses.

3. Recruiting external, non-cyber security candidates is also an option.

4. Successes have included hiring college grads without technical majors, armed services veterans, and young adults without college degrees.

CHAPTER 06

EMPLOYEE VALUE PROPOSITION – PROPOSING THE PROPOSITION

In this chapter, we will define an employee value proposition and teach you how to make one for every role that you're working on.

Every couple of weeks, I will get an email or LinkedIn message from a recruiter asking me if I'm interested in a new opportunity to work as a cyber security recruiter for their company. The email will read something like this:

Subject: Exciting Opportunity

Hi Renee,

Our company is building out its HR team and has an exciting opportunity for a technical recruiter who is looking to take her career to the next level. There has never been a more urgent time to obtain the best talent we can for an area so critical to our organization.

We have a great working environment and total rewards package. Let's connect if you're interested.

Regards,

Emily

Most of the times I ignore these messages, but occasionally I will take a look at the job description that is posted and the job description almost always looks the same. It will be something generic explaining what the company is seeking in a candidate. It will usually have a laundry list of required and desired. It's like I could look at 5 different job descriptions for roles in a bunch of different companies and they would all say the same thing.

If I'm gainfully and happily employed, why would I even look at these job descriptions and entertain having a conversation with a recruiter, when they all look the same? As far as I can see, from the job description, there is nothing exciting about the opportunity. It's the same old stuff.

Now, I get a message like that once every few weeks. Imagine being bombarded with dozens of messages like that every day. Welp! I would probably just do mass deletes, unless something was so intriguing that I had to read more.

This is what's happening when you reach out to a cyber security professional with a generic message and a bogus job description.

Your job description and job posting suck

Think about your favorite ads on social media, email, or TV. The headline is eye catching, and the images make you want to know more about the product or service. Your job posting should have some elements of this. Maybe you can't add a flashy picture, however, the headline should be catchy and the job posting should provide an employee value proposition.

What's an employee value proposition?

According to a recent Gallup article, an employee value proposition (EVP) – which is closely related to the concept of a company's employment brand – articulates the balance of the rewards and benefits that employees collect in return for what they contribute to a workplace.

Apple came up with a perfect EVP when they announced full education reimbursement for its employees. It developed its current workforce, and additionally attracted the innovative types of employees who are continuously learning. It confirmed what the company values.

In a nutshell, Apple's EVP appeals to the right kind of people – those who want to learn and grow and who are likely to be engaged with Apple's development-oriented culture.

What does your company, or team, provide that is a differentiator? Every company can't compete with Apple. And that's fine. But we want you to stand out from your competitors. This can be done by providing information about the team, the projects, the work environments, the fringe benefits and perks, and anything else that makes your company stand out from others.

This is the kind of information that needs to go in your job description.

Why should I work for you?

I am working with a Fortune 500 company right now on a cyber security recruiting project. They are doing a major cloud migration and transferring thousands of apps into the cloud using AWS. This is the largest migration in terms of scale to date. The hiring manager and HR team did an awesome job drafting a job description that shares the scope of the project. This skill set is new, in-demand and difficult to find. There is zero unemployment in this space. When I call a candidate and say that I'm working on a role for this company and this is "the largest AWS migration of its kind to date", they are intrigued. This is a compelling EVP.

The folks who are interested in these roles aren't interested based on the company's benefits or perks. They want to say they worked on a project that "is the largest migration to date". This is what you need from your managers on the roles that you're working on. What is compelling about the job that you're working on? Is the hiring manager a rockstar in the field? Some people want to work for certain people. I remember working for a woman who was known to be extremely difficult to work for. I made the decision to work for her because she was "the best in the business" at the time, and I wanted to learn from her.

What else can you sell about the role, team, environment, etc? Does the manager allow team members extra time to work on side projects? Do they encourage continuous learning and growing? After the project is over, what can the candidate expect to do next to grow their skills?

Think about what the person will be able to take to their next employer or project when they are done working with your company. I recently worked on a recruiting project where I helped a team hire a manager in a company that needed a total technology upgrade. This company was doing everything manually and the operations were like an episode of Mad Men. Computers were used sporadically and not much information was shared across the team. I helped the company draft an EVP. The EVP was that this person would be able to use their knowledge of the best practices to "install new systems from scratch and greatly improve efficiencies". This was a compelling EVP.

The person we hired was excited for the challenge to get his hands dirty and build this new environment from scratch. I told him that he could take the knowledge from this experience as a resume builder and that his next employer would see that he was a "turnaround guy". This is how we convinced a millennial with major corporate experience to take a role in a small company without a networked computer system!

Going back to the actual job description, have you ever thought of an infographic for your job description? I can almost guarantee that it would get many more responses and shares than the standard written templates that are out there now.

Why your EVP must be the truth

Some companies tend to inflate their EVP. They set expectations of a certain environment and then when the person is hired, the role is not as described. This is the fastest way to set your recruiting efforts up for failure, because your new hire will walk right out the door. Because most of these cyber security employees have people beating down their door to hire them, they are much less likely to stay in a situation that wasn't presented correctly. Your goal should be to hire someone who will stay in the role for at least a year. Sometimes turnover is inevitable and there is nothing that can be done on the front end, however, more often than not, there is some miscommunication in the initial phase of the hiring process that leads to a person leaving prematurely.

When speaking with candidates on a daily basis, one of the top reasons they will look to leave their current situation is because the role that was described during the interview process is not what they're doing on a daily basis. Most realize that business needs change and roles can morph, but they are less likely to stick around in a hot market like this one when some other recruiter is chomping at the bit for them to be interested in hearing about their newest opportunity.

This was another fascinating aspect of me sitting next to some really technical folks in cyber security. I remember having conversations with some of my colleagues about their frustrations with their work - that the projects they had been hired to work on were stalled and they were getting frustrated. Having been in various corporate environments, this was standard operating procedure for me. Many times projects were stalled, and we just waited for them to be back on the front burners. Was this frustrating? Absolutely. Was it a reason for me to quit? No way. Well I got a rude awakening because for these highly skilled people, a stalled project and frustration meant that their skills were getting stagnant, and they were ready to move on. Quite often they would complain on a Monday, and in the next few weeks they were giving in their resignations. Wow!

I would think of my former self in HR trying to figure out why there was so much turnover in certain information security groups. This was the reason! These employees very much want to improve and grow their skills. Because technologies change so quickly, staying stagnant is not an option. If a project is delayed for too long and the employee is not put on another project where they can learn and grow their skills, they will leave. This is why retention is as important, or even more important, than recruiting. You can view case studies of companies with great EVPs at **magnetichiring.com**.

KEY TAKEAWAYS

1. An employee value proposition (EVP) is needed for every role that you recruit for.

2. Even if your company has an EVP that talks about the overall company's total rewards, you will need one specific to the group, team, and position.

3. Use an intriguing job description to get talent interested in your job.

4. An EVP should tell the candidate why he should consider your job opening.

5. Keep your EVP honest in order to retain the talent that you recruit.

CHAPTER 07

CREATIVE SOURCING

When I'm working with clients, they often ask me how I can find talent that seems unattainable to them. Or, they can find the talent, but the people won't respond to them. They wonder how I can get a response from candidates that they've been trying to reach for a long time. Here I will outline the best ways to reach your desired candidates.

Where do they hang out?

Online, they are in a number of places. Some have their own blogs, or they write or share articles on LinkedIn. They will also participate in LinkedIn groups. Some are on Twitter. Others are doing extra projects or asking questions in online communities like Github or Stack Overflow. They may also be part of online university and employer alumni networks.

Offline, they are at security conferences that are held around the country all the time. On any given week, there are dozens of security conferences happening and if your company has the budget, you can request that they become a sponsor at some of these events. You could also just ask for your company to sponsor you as an attendee, and you can mingle with the cyber security professionals there. Listening to the presentations is a great way to learn about what's hot in the industry and ask compelling questions. Some may attend career fairs but mostly as part of a conference. They don't really need to go to a physical career fair when they are being bombarded by job opportunities. You can find a list of the biggest cyber conferences at **magnetichiring.com**.

They're always at work! If you get their corporate email and phone number, you have direct access to them. E-mail and LinkedIn are my go-to ways to reach out to candidates. I typically send e-mails and get responses almost immediately that way.

How to reach out to them

There really isn't a magic way to reach people. Most of the time, if you send an intriguing e-mail or LinkedIn message, you will get a yes or no response. If the person you're trying to connect with isn't interested in new opportunities at this time, you can ask for a referral.

To view some sample emails that I've used to get results, visit magnetichiring.com.

Connecting with your candidates

Rebecca sent out over a hundred e-mails to candidates for an incident response manager position she was working on. She started getting responses back and scheduled some phone calls to speak with the potential candidates about their careers and her opportunity.

Her first call was with John. She did a quick LinkedIn review and Google search to see what John was up to. She saw that he recently won an award for his company for going above and beyond on a recent incident. She also saw that he was scheduled to speak at one of the upcoming conferences. She jotted down these notes as she picked up the phone to call John.

Rebecca started the conversation by thanking John for his time. She congratulated him on his recent award. She told him she saw from his LinkedIn profile that he was doing amazing things for his company and they seemed to be rewarding him for them. John was excited to talk about his recent award. He began to tell her about what he had done to achieve the award. There was an incident, and he and the team spent the entire weekend triaging to get it under control. The leadership team took notice and gave him and his team awards.

She then asked him if he was even interested in exploring other opportunities since it seemed like he had a great situation where he was. He said he was always open to new things. Rebecca asked more questions about his day-to-day activities and the accomplishments he was most proud of. She listened intently and took copious notes. She restated some of his main points to make sure she got it right and told him about her role. She believed that with his current skills and experience, he would be a huge asset to the company. She also shared some of the company and project benefits that seemed to match his interests. He told her she was one of the few recruiters that "got him" and he'd be happy to continue the conversation and move forward with next steps.

She wished him luck on his upcoming speech at next week's cyber security conference, and he told her he was nervous to speak in front of such a large crowd. Rebecca was confident that this candidate would move forward in the process.

Sourcing approach

Rebecca's approach was spot on. She quickly gained rapport with the candidate and listened to his wants. She then provided her company's EVP and highlighted the areas that matched what he was seeking next in his career. It seems like a no-brainer but many recruiters aren't taking these steps. Below, I outline what you should do after your email request is accepted.

When someone does respond to your request, the first thing you need to do is Google them to find out what they're doing in their field. Do they have a blog? What are they tweeting? Have they spoken at a recent conference? Ideally, you would have the time to research people prior to reaching out but I realize that time is of the essence, and sometimes you'll need to search people based on their current or past job titles and some key words.

You'll want to have a few key talking points that you can bring up about their background. People respect the fact that you have done some due diligence before reaching out to them. If they just spoke at a conference, you don't have to watch the entire thing but if you listen for a couple points they made over

10-15 minutes, you can bring that up. Just doing this will put you head and shoulders above most recruiters out there.

Then you'll want to dangle your carrot. You'll tell the person that you have an opportunity that you'd like to share, and you'd like to hear about their current situation and what they'd like to do next in their career. This will get them talking to you about their career aspirations and you'll be able to gauge if your opportunity will be a fit.

For example, let's say you're recruiting for a role that is 70% travel and you hear the person say that she is traveling like crazy right now and wants to cut back. Clearly this position is not the right fit. You don't want to try and shove it down her throat. Be honest and say that the role you have is 70% travel so you don't think there'd be a fit, but you can give more details if she'd like to hear more. And you'd like to hear more about her because you have new opportunities daily.

Most people will respect that you are not pressuring them. There are so many different recruiters calling on them and treating them like cattle that they will be pleasantly surprised that you actually know a little bit about them and that you realize when the opportunity won't be a fit. Many will ask your opinion on the market and will reach out months later to reconnect when they are ready to make a move. You'll have to remember that this is a marathon and not a race. The folks who aren't interested in your roles now may call you in six months, and your role may still be open or you have new ones that may be a fit. When you do what's in the best interest of both the company and the candidate, you'll always be a step ahead of everyone else.

It's a numbers game...but no one wants to feel like a number

Rebecca sent out over 100 e-mails with the exact same message. Maybe she tweaked one or two based on something she saw in their profile, but overall, she sent out a mass e-mail. The e-mails were targeted though. She sent them out to people who had the criteria she was seeking - or at least they looked like they had the criteria based on her key word searches.

The key to making everyone feel like the message is written only for them is to do some due diligence on their background. This makes a huge difference with the way you are viewed by the candidate. Remember the pop star analogy. How would you prepare to get on the phone with Adele's or Rihanna's team? You would Google them and see what's going on with their career. You'd listen to some of their music. You'd check to see their latest projects and on and on. I'm not saying that you have to go this in depth. There are only so many hours in a day. However, you must do some preliminary research prior to getting on the phone so you don't sound like every other person trying to reach them.

Quality and speed

When you reach out to candidates the way I outlined, you'll get better results faster. This will help with your relationships with your hiring managers. They will feel confident that you can get them the best talent and you can get it to them quickly.

As discussed in a prior chapter, when a manager is filling a position, they are doing their own job and stretching their team by having them pick up the slack. They want to see results from you. You will need to set their expectations that it typically takes two weeks to start seeing a slate of qualified candidates. You're not manufacturing people. You have to do outreach, get people on the phone, and get them interested. Remind them that these are people and not just "resumes". Managers tend to ask for resumes, and I always correct them and say candidates. These are not just pieces of paper that I get from a database. These are people who you've had conversations with who could be a match for the position.

KEY TAKEAWAYS

1. The fastest way to connect with a cyber security professional is to email them at work.

2. They also hang out offline at cyber security conferences and meetups.

3. Research the candidate prior to having a phone call with them. Understand their most recent accomplishments and find out what they're looking to do next in their careers.

CHAPTER 08

TRUST THE PROCESS – SEAL THE DEAL

In this chapter, I will teach you how to prep managers to interview and how to set up the offer so you have a higher rate of acceptance.

Marvin, the hiring manager, had a great interview with Quinn. After her interview, he walked away thinking she would be an asset to the team. Not only were Quinn's technical skills up to par but also her soft skills would definitely help their team since some of the other team members tended to be rough around the edges. Marvin reached out to the team members to see what they thought of Quinn. Everyone thought she would be great.

Marvin's recruiter, Malcolm, calls him to get feedback on Quinn. Marvin thought she was awesome and she would fit great with the team. Perfect. Malcolm started talking numbers with Marvin.

He figured Marvin wanted to put together an offer for Quinn. Marvin told Malcolm that although he thought she was great, he wanted to see more people in order to make a decision.

Malcolm was annoyed. He explained to Marvin that he may not get another Quinn and why would he risk losing a candidate that the entire team thought was a fit just so he could look around and see what else was out there. Marvin insisted and the search continued.

Malcolm rushed to get him some other people to interview, but it still took a few weeks. In the meantime, Malcolm called Quinn to let her know they were still very much interested in her but had to finish some other interviews that they had started. Quinn shared that she was very much still interested in the role and to continue to keep her posted.

While Marvin was interviewing other candidates to see if they measured up to Quinn, Quinn was going on more interviews since she didn't have an offer in hand. Quinn was an amazing candidate, and she received multiple offers as the days passed.

When Marvin finally got his act together to offer Quinn the job, she had already accepted another role. She told Marvin that she thought he and his team were great but figured they weren't interested since they continued their search.

Time kills deals...a bird in the hand is better than two in the bush

This scenario happens more often than not. A hiring manager thinks that there's a better person out there for his role. There very well may be better people out there, but the question will be whether they are willing to take that job.

This is where your role as a recruiter becomes trusted advisor. Prior to scheduling interviews, you will need to have a conversation with your hiring manager around decision-making on the candidates. The manager will need to make a decision on a hire relatively quickly. As soon as someone is interviewed, the manager and team should be able to make a decision - even if the decision is maybe. You should give your hiring manager scenarios where managers have lost candidates due to time and indecisiveness. Let them know that it may be difficult to make a decision to hire someone based on the first candidate, however, the person is being evaluated against the criteria of the role and not against each other. It's ideal when a manager has multiple people to compare and contrast but if the candidate is exactly what they're seeking, they need to make an offer quickly.

Even if they decide to try and complete a few additional interviews to compare, they should do those immediately. They can't wait weeks while they go through candidate resumes in painstaking detail and expect that a candidate who's as sharp as the person they met would be still available.

It's easy to equate it to the housing market. Tell your manager to imagine they are looking for a house. They find the exact house that they want with all of their requirements, in the perfect location, and it's within their desired price range. Are they going to wait two weeks to view other homes and see how they compare? Or, would they quickly check out some other homes to really see if they remotely measured up, and then put an offer on that first house as soon as possible? They would probably go with option two. It's understandable to want to see what's out there, but you better do so quickly or your favorite house will be off the market.

The interview team is key

Joe, a security engineer, had been contacted by Mary about an opening at her company. She shared all the benefits and the EVP to Joe, and he thought the role could help him in the next leg of his career. Mary explained the process to him. She would forward along his credentials and would wait to hear back on next steps. If all went well, he would do a phone interview and technical screening. He would then come into the office for a face-to-face or Skype meeting.

Joe's first interview was a bust. The interviewer, Robert, had him aligned to a different role than what was discussed with the recruiter. Joe wasn't remotely interested in that role and he shared that with Robert. Joe asked Robert some questions about the role that he was unable to answer, and eventually, they ended the conversation. Robert thought Joe had no interest in the role and couldn't quite understand why he was even passed along into the interview pipeline.

Joe's feedback was that the manager couldn't answer his questions and quite frankly he wasn't interested in the role that they advertised. Joe said that they were disorganized and couldn't get their act together. This experience is a sour one and a lesson that needed to be learned for the management team but unfortunately, the candidate now looks at this company with disdain.

The interview team is key to recruiting. In the initial strategy session, you want to emphasize that the recruiting team is key and that you want to put your best interviewing team members on the case. If you can work with the manager to ensure that he has the right interviewing team, that's ideal.

Offers will be turned down

One of the biggest eye openers for me recruiting cyber security professionals is that you can extend offers and they may not be accepted, and you have to be OK with that scenario. Recruiting 101 teaches that your candidates should be "locked up" prior to moving forward in the process. "Locked up" meaning that you've ensured that they are willing to take the position if the offer extended is what they were seeking.

This is not the case in security. You will need to extend many offers and people will turn them down. It's the nature of working in a competitive hiring market. Don't get emotional about it. Be prepared to extend multiple offers and do your best to close them, but realize that each of these candidates have multiple offers on the table, so someone will get turned down.

KEY TAKEAWAYS

1. Coach your hiring team on how to interview and give them answers to FAQs.

2. Prepare your hiring manager to be decisive about offering the right candidate a position.

3. Offers will be turned down in this type of market. Prep your manager for this.

CHAPTER 09

MY WISH FOR YOU

Michelle had been my client for six months when she started asking me in depth questions about different techniques for recruiting cyber security talent. Her company was using me as their go-to staffing firm for their difficult-to-fill cyber security searches. Prior to engaging me, they had struggled for almost a year to fill multiple security positions. After consistently bringing her a slate of qualified, interested candidates, she wanted me to give her the inside scoop on how my team worked. I had an awesome partnership with Michelle and had already been coaching her since she had been asking me questions along the way with the various roles that I helped her fill.

I made Michelle aware of a training program that I run for recruiters who want to learn from me as to how to recruit their own cyber security talent. I told her that I would be giving her my personal handbook on how to fill these challenging positions and all of the tactics that I use to find the right talent and get them interested in these roles. Michelle shared this info with her manager, and her manager signed up their technical recruiting team to work with me.

I walked Michelle and her peers step by step through each open position that they had. I coached them prior to meeting with their hiring managers. If they need an updated EVP for each role, we did that. If we needed to adjust the skill set, I coached them on how to have those conversations with the hiring managers. She and her peers were at different stages in the process, so I worked with each of them individually and then in a group setting.

The recruiters immediately felt empowered since they knew that they had an expert who could give them the exact verbiage and email templates to use while speaking with both their hiring managers and the candidates. They became more confident after they used some of the same resources that I've shared with you on **magnetichiring.com**.

A few weeks after the training began, the recruiters started to see the fruits of their labor. They had qualified candidates interested in the positions that they were trying to fill. The hiring managers felt confident that the recruitment team understood what they were seeking and that their positions would be filled quickly.

In the first month after the recruiters started working with me, they were able to extend the first of many offers to candidates for cyber security roles. And they got some accepted offers! The team was ecstatic. They had finally begun to crack the code to attracting and hiring cyber security talent to their organization.

After working with the recruitment team month after month, they became better at overcoming all the challenges they dealt with before. Michelle got a promotion to lead the newly developed cyber recruitment team that consisted of recruiters, sourcers, and coordinators, solely dedicated to dealing with the cyber openings. This was a huge accomplishment for the HR team and showed how a group could become trusted advisors and a huge asset to the organization.

Obstacles

There are many pieces to recruiting cyber security professionals that I described over the course of this book. You can follow the instructions step by step, and you may get a perfect outcome. You can also make one small hiccup and that can unravel everything that you've worked so hard to achieve.

You can have the best process laid out for getting the talent and do everything that I outlined in this book, and your hiring manager can have some underlying challenges that you aren't aware of and put a monkey wrench in the entire plan.

You could be dealing with corporate bureaucracy and getting blocked at every turn for moving the process forward. You could also have your own blind spots that you're unable to see because you are deeply entrenched in the process.

If you're working with a headhunter or an agency recruiter, utilize their expertise. They are seeing these scenarios happening with an array of clients on a daily basis. If they give nuggets of information, share them with your hiring manager. Ensure that your hiring manager has access to the headhunter. You don't need to know everything. Let them make you shine.

If any of these obstacles come up, and you don't have a trainer or mentor in cyber recruiting to bounce ideas off of, how will you know that you're moving in the right direction and going down the right path. It's very difficult going through this process alone when you don't know the answers and have no one to ask questions.

The clients that work with our team get immediate results and they are usually able to fill roles that had been open for months within 30-60 days. Even if you don't work with our team, find a trainer who has extensive experience in dealing with cyber security professionals. A standard tech recruiting class won't do. It has to be focused in cyber security.

It has been a fun ride sharing the inside tips of the fascinating world of cyber security recruiting. It's a difficult challenge to overcome but once you do so, you will have the leaders of your organization singing your praises and giving you more opportunities to show off your amazing problem solving skills.

You will be able to have a consultative relationship with the cyber security leaders and start to focus on helping them to retain their staff, which is really the bigger issue. It's one thing to work as hard as you just did to find them the staff that they needed. It's a total nightmare when that person leaves within a few months because their expectations weren't set correctly. This is where you can add tremendous value to your team and earn a permanent spot with the leaders of your organization.

RESOURCES

http://www.ioti.com/security/how-train-cybersecurity-professionals-future

https://www.forbes.com/sites/jeffkauflin/2017/03/16/the-fast-growing-job-with-a-huge-skills-gap-cyber-security/#47607cf75163

http://cyberseek.org/index.html

http://blog.indeed.com/2017/01/17/cybersecurity-skills-gap-report/

http://www.reuters.com/article/us-jpmorgan-cybersecurity-idUSKCN0HR23T20141003

http://www.csoonline.com/article/3075293/leadership-management/cybersecurity-recruitment-in-crisis.html

http://www.csoonline.com/article/3110146/it-careers/the-best-places-to-live-for-cybersecurity-jobs-that-pay.html#slide4

http://www.workforce.com/2016/05/09/hr-and-it-the-dynamic-duo-in-cybersecurity/

http://www.crainsnewyork.com/article/20150503/TECHNOLOGY/150509977/new-york-citys-newest-rock-stars-the-it-boys

http://www.zdnet.com/article/cybersecurity-hiring-crisis-rockstars-anger-and-the-billion-dollar-problem/

http://fortune.com/2016/01/13/pwc-tech-talent-shortage/

http://www.cnbc.com/2016/02/26/giving-veterans-a-new-start-in-cybersecurity.html

https://www.symantec.com/about/corporate-responsibility/your-information/cyber-career-connection

ACKNOWLEDGEMENTS

I was inspired to write a book about recruiting cyber security professionals since the time I overcame this challenge five years ago. I felt the **need** to write this book after becoming the CEO of an HR consulting company focused on cyber security staffing and retention because I wanted to help my fellow former corporate recruiter clients overcome the challenges they had been facing with recruiting cyber security talent. I wanted to tell them that they were making it harder on themselves that they needed to be. This process could be seamless and they could attract more of the specific talent that they were seeking if they followed some easy steps.

I want to acknowledge all of the cyber security professionals and hiring managers who let me pick their brains over the course of my time recruiting for them. I also thank my clients, the cyber security recruiters, that share their challenges and keep me close to their day-to-day struggles.

ABOUT THE AUTHOR

Renee Brown Small is a cyber security recruitment expert. She has been recruiting technology professionals since 2001. As the founder and CEO of Cyber Human Capital, Renee consults with companies to improve their cyber security hiring process and provides customized cyber security recruiter training. She holds a BS in Information Systems from the Stern School of Business at New York University. She lives in McLean, VA with her husband and three children.

THANK YOU

Thank you for reading this book. As shared throughout the book, there are multiple resources to help you get through the process of recruiting your next cyber security professional at **www.magnetichiring.com**

I hope this book and the resources make your next recruit easier than your last.

I created a note that you can write to your boss to let them know that you read this book and would love to attend the training course that will give you the fast track to getting your cyber security roles filled quickly and seamlessly. Sign up to get this at **www.magnetichiring.com**

ABOUT DIFFERENCE PRESS

difference press

Difference Press offers entrepreneurs, including life coaches, healers, consultants, and community leaders, a comprehensive solution to get their books written, published, and promoted. A boutique-style alternative to self-publishing, Difference Press boasts a fair and easy-to-understand profit structure, low-priced author copies, and author-friendly contract terms. Its founder, Dr. Angela Lauria, has been bringing to life the literary ventures of hundreds of authors-in-transformation since 1994.

LET'S MAKE A DIFFERENCE WITH YOUR BOOK

You've seen other people make a difference with a book. Now it's your turn. If you are ready to stop watching and start taking massive action, reach out.

"Yes, I'm ready!"

In a market where hundreds of thousands books are published every year and are never heard from again, all participants of The Author Incubator have bestsellers that are actively changing lives and making a difference.

"In two years we've created over 250 bestselling books in a row, 90% from first-time authors." We do this by selecting the highest quality and highest potential applicants for our future programs.

Our program doesn't just teach you how to write a book—our team of coaches, developmental editors, copy editors, art directors, and marketing experts incubate you from book idea to published bestseller, ensuring that the book you create can actually make a difference in the world. Then we give you the training you need to use your book to make the difference you want to make in the world, or to create a business out of serving your readers. If you have life-or world-changing ideas or services, a servant's heart, and the willingness to do what it REALLY takes to make a difference in the world with your book, go to http://theauthorincubator.com/apply/ to complete an application for the program today.

OTHER BOOKS BY DIFFERENCE PRESS

Help! My Kid Wants to Become a Youtuber

by Michael Buckley and Jess Malhotra

...But I'm Not Racist!: Tools for Well-Meaning Whites

by Kathy Obear

Pride: You Can't Heal If You're Hiding from Yourself

by Ron Holt

The Face of the Business: Develop Your Signature Style, Step Out from Behind the Curtain and Catapult Your Business on Video

by Rachel Nachmias

Urban Ecology: A Natural Way to Transform Kids, Parks, Cities, and the World

by Ken Leinbach

Why Can't I Drink Like Everyone Else?: A Step-By-Step Guide to Understanding Why You Drink and Knowing How to Take a Break

by Rachel Hart

Finding Time to Lead: Seven Practices to Unleash Outrageous Potential

by Leslie Peters

Standing Up: From Renegade Professor to Middle-Aged Comic

by Ada Cheng

Flex Mom: The Secrets of Happy Stay-At-Home Moms

by Sara Blanchard

Your First CFO: The Accounting Cure for Small Business Owners

by Pam Prior

Just Tell Me What I Want: How to Find Your Purpose When You Have No Idea What It Is

by Sara Kravitz

From Sidelines to Start Lines: The Frustrated Runner's Guide to Lacing Up for a Lifetime

by Sarah Richardson

Everyday Medium: 7 Steps to Discover, Develop and Direct Your Sixth Sense

by Marsha Farias

Think Again!: Clearing Away the Brain Fog of Menopause

by Jeanne Andrus

Relationship Detox: 7 Steps to Prepare for Your Ideal Relationship

by Jodi Schuelke

Unclutter Your Spirit: How Your Stuff is a Treasure Map to Your Inner Wisdom

by Sue Rasmussed

Made in the USA
Columbia, SC
15 August 2020